THE OLD COASTLINE

For Pamela

I hope you
find something
good and lovely
in these poems

Much love,

Fred

The Old Coastline

SELECTED POEMS OF
M. VASALIS

TRANSLATED BY FRED LESSING
& DAVID YOUNG

PINYON PUBLISHING
Montrose, Colorado

Original Works:

Parken en woestijnen, De vogel Phoenix, Vergezichten en gezichten,
& De oude kustlijn

Copyright © by M. Vasalis, Amsterdam

First published by Uitgeverij Van Oorschot

Published by special arrangement with Uitgeverij Van Oorschot in conjunction with their duly appointed agent, 2 Seas Literary Agency

Translations Copyright © 2019 by Fred Lessing & David Young

Cover painting "Vasalis" by Joke Bijnsdorp
50 cm x 60 cm, oil on canvas, 2012

Design by Susan Entsminger

First Edition: March 2019

Pinyon Publishing
23847 V66 Trail, Montrose, CO 81403
www.pinyon-publishing.com

Library of Congress Control Number: 2019936135
ISBN: 978-1-936671-55-7

ACKNOWLEDGMENTS

Some of these translations appeared previously in the following periodicals: *Miramar, Plume,* and *Pinyon Review.*

CONTENTS

APPENDIX

INTRODUCTIONS

I

M. Vasalis (1909-1998) was the pen name of Margaretha Drooglever-Fortuyn-Leenmans, a Dutch psychiatrist who specialized in children. Vasalis has been, and remains, one of the most widely read and admired poets of her language and country, despite a relative obscurity on the international poetry scene. Something of a loner, she did not spend time in literary circles and had very little interest in promoting her work and career. Her poems come out of her life, her experience of the natural world, her professional practice, and her family relations. They arise from the pressure of occasion and necessity rather than from an ambition to originality or greatness, but their relative modesty is one of their secret strengths. They may not have grand designs on literary tradition or destiny, but their clarity of vision and expression, their honesty about emotions and common human dilemmas, have made them invaluable to readers.

One friend who knows her work well has called her "the Dutch Elizabeth Bishop," and that characterization is helpful. These are poems that readers cherish for their intensity and intimacy. If Whitman and Dickinson are familiar polarities, Vasalis is much closer to the Dickinson pole, though in her case we have a poet who was more cinematic in her effects and who was widely read from early on in her career.

Reflecting changes in literary practice as well as natural development, her style over the years grows less formal and more immediate. Her expertise with rhyme and meter, evident in her first volume, *Parken en woestijnen* (*Parks and Deserts*), 1940, is never abandoned, but she handles it more distinctively and less self-consciously as the years go by. There is a publishing hiatus in her career, marked both by World War Two and by the loss of a child to illness. Her second collection, *De vogel Phoenix* (*The Phoenix Bird*) did not appear until 1947; it is dedicated to the dead child Dicky, who lived just a year and a half. The poems of grief that open this collection are among the most moving and deeply considered examples I know.

A third collection, *Vergezichten en gezichten* (*Views and Visages*), appeared in 1954, and there was a posthumous volume, *De oude kustlijn* (*The Old Coastline*), in 2002. Many of those late poems are untitled. They often deal with love, with the raising of children, and with the woes of illness, both physical and mental. Always nature can provide some solace, but there are no final answers to suffering and loss. Her deepening of subject and treatment make her arc of development a powerful example that readers can follow by means of our chronological organization.

Vasalis' directness and accessibility make her easy and delightful to translate, but issues of tone, because of the complexity of her insights and the delicacy of her touch, keep translators challenged and cautious. Our collaboration has been essential to solving these problems, and we like to think that together we have gone to places no single translator might have been capable of reaching. I have known Fred Lessing since our college days, when we were roommates, and his psychological insights – he was for many years a practicing therapist – have helped immensely in aligning the English versions I have fashioned with their Dutch originals. I think Vasalis would have enjoyed our translation partnership, speaking as it does to her modesty, her immense human sympathies, her bonds with the natural world, and the precision with which she tracks her insights as she grows older and wiser.

—David Young

II

I am a Holocaust survivor, psychotherapist and retired professor of philosophy who managed to retain knowledge and use of my native Dutch language after immigrating to America at age 12, as well as my warm friendship with David Young, my college roommate. I had no knowledge of Vasalis or her poetry until some years ago when my two brothers asked whether I, like the two of them, knew and admired the poem "De idioot in het bad".

Reading it moved me deeply. I remember being struck simultaneously by its clarity and its empathy, not a feeling of having just read a poem about a boy with Down Syndrome but rather one of presence, of having been in the room with him, seeing and hearing him, even knowing him and feeling his feelings and caring deeply about him as though he were my child.

Of course it wasn't real, yet it moved me and the more I studied it, the more it seemed to me inspired by the same muse as much of David's poetry. I wanted to share it with him and was pretty sure he would also really like it and appreciate the author's skills and sensibility and I turned out to be right about that. But since he did not speak or read Dutch I would have to provide him with a translation and that became my first serious engagement with the many complexities, problems and difficult decisions of the world of poetry translation. It was a rough literal version I produced but good enough for David to be able to transform it into one that does justice to Vasalis' original. It pleased both of us and triggered in both of us, I think, a sense of having struck gold and a shared desire to translate more of this poet's amazing poems. This book is the happy and humble culmination of what became the goal of this project: to make Vasalis' wonderful work available to English-speaking lovers of poetry. It has been, as clearly Vasalis' poems are and perhaps all poetry is, a labor of love: love of poetry, love of the two-poled process of translation, love of Vasalis and everything she loved and touched upon and, for us probably most of all, the love that inheres in our friendship.

—*Fred Lessing*

From

Parks and Deserts (1940)

DRINK, THE UNPREDICTABLE

Under the genteel, fluent talk
my brown-hat head's supposed
to carry on, conversing with my host,
my whole soul's thinking, *Awk!*
Inside me animals stampede,
woods rustle, horses snort and toss,
snakes go slithering through moss,
and tribes of natives celebrate and breed.
Port or sherry … rather have tea?
Yes ma'am, or actually no, not me.
Stark naked I dive into a lake.
Just half full please … that's all that I can take!
How in God's name can I go on speaking …
Do they notice I'm unsteady?
Have my ears turned red already?
Can I hold my liquor without leaking?
Suppose we try to shave that cat
that consolation prize, that poodle-rat
with frost on his backside, below me.
Nobody knows how terribly wild,
hair all loose, I walk and run.
Nobody here would know me
if I were suddenly flayed,
because they only know my skin,
and only parts of that displayed.
Oh brown and modest bride, so mild,
out of Tahiti or the Philippines …
it's getting dark in here; outside
snow flutters silently and falls
on shrubs that are light green.

DEATH

Death showed me small and interesting things:
this is a nail – Death said – and this is a rope.
I gaze at him, a child. He's my master
because I admire him and trust him,
Death.

He showed it all to me: drink, pills,
guns, gas cock, pitched roofs,
bath-tub, razor blade, white sheet
"no reason" – in case someday I'd want
death.

And before he left, he gave me a little portrait …
"I don't know if you'd forget,
but it might come in handy someday
when after all you might not want
to die,
but, who's stopping you?"
said Death.

THE IDIOT IN THE BATH

Trotting and almost tripping on the mat,
Held by his nurse, unable to speak,
Shoulders hunched up and eyes squeezed shut,
The idiot goes to his bath each week.

Mist from the water rises, spreads,
Calms him and reassures: white steam ...
Each piece of clothing that he sheds
Brings him closer to a trusted dream.

She eases him in; across his chest
He folds thin arms, his breathing slows,
And he sighs, as if he had quenched a great thirst,
While round his mouth a look of pleasure glows.

His anxious face is handsome now, quite blank,
His thin feet stand like flowers – pale, serene –,
His long blanched legs, withered a bit, and lank,
Are like young birch trunks glimpsed amidst the green.

In this green water he has yet to happen,
He need not know that some fruits never ripen.
His body has the wisdom it requires.
His mind can lose the world and its desires.

And when he's taken out, and toweled dry,
And dressed again in stiff, hard clothes,
He fights and weeps, resisting with his cries,
That world outside to which he always goes.

Each week he is reborn to painful matters,
Each week, for him, the same fate lies in store:
Harshly removed from his life-giving waters,
To be a frightened idiot once more.

TIME

I dreamed that I lived slowly, all alone,
lived slower than the oldest stone.

And it was terrible: all round me
things that seem still to us shot up,
shivering, writhing. I saw the urgency
with which trees wrung themselves
out of the earth, while they sang hoarsely,
haltingly, and seasons fell and rose
more fleetingly than rainbows ...

I saw the tremor of the sea,
the way it swells and quickly sinks,
almost the way a large throat drinks.

And day and night went by, so quick,
flaring and winking out, a fire-flick.

Such eloquence and such despair
in all that gesturing of things
that normally hold still, their crowd and press,
their breathless, cruel and endless contest ...

How is it that I did not get it
sooner, not see all that
in former times? And now,
how will I ever forget it?

SPRING

The light gusts across the land in spurts,
waking the hard, brief glitter
of the blue, wind-ruffled ditches and canals;
the grass lights up, dims down, goes dark.
Two newborn lambs next to a grizzled sheep
stand white, printing youth's picture against grass.
I had forgotten how this was, and that
the spring is not a quiet blossoming,
dreaming softly, but a violent growing,
a pure and passionate beginning,
jumping up out of a deep sleep,
and dancing away without a thought.

THE FUNERAL OF MRS. T.

Along the narrow, wooded, rising lane
we waded slowly, following her coffin.
Our throats were sore from being silent,
from trying to match her quiet reticence.

Eight somber strangers, blackly dressed,
doing those things that are done stiffly, last ...
Such a small grave, a black wedge of dirt,
a thin wound in the glistening green earth.

And on that grass, profoundly, the sun shone
because of the good mother she had been.
Almost happy, everything fragrant and sun-bright,
almost dead, if I thought what was going on ...
After some soft and flagging conversation,
we left, and let her be alone.

THE TREK

One evening, sitting on a railing,
I watched a *trek* approaching.
Four donkeys trotted first, on silent hooves.
A black and bearded billy-goat came next,
and led a group of motley she-goats past.
The little two-wheeled cart brought up the rear,
its horses turning round to bite the air
behind them angrily, and then go on –
and on the cart, with her two mute and staring sons,
a swarthy wife. Their three heads turned
to watch me as they floated by
so unencumbered and so tranquilly …
I watched them go and thought I'd like to be
that peaceful too, that homeless, and that free.

LITTLE DONKEY

In the twilight that was fading
I did a little quiet walking.
The earth was dry and cracked and red,
the air was thin, all altitude;
blue thistles, stiff and bristling,
set up a hostile rustling.
Beside a boulder, suddenly,
I spied a youthful grazing donkey;
his ears, translucent, glowed,
his countenance was proud,
his eyes were large and amber,
and thoughtful, like still water;
he did not judge me with his gaze.
I startled first, then stood amazed
and felt a kind of reverence for
this unspoiled, lovely creature,
as I continued slowly on my way.
Now it's a painful memory.
I know that I was like that once,
all dignity and innocence,
grave but not heavy, dreamy, bright:
if I could just regain that state,
could just begin again, and be
what that donkey was to me ...

ENCLOSURE DIKE

The bus rides through the night, a quiet room,
the road is straight, the dike is endless;
the sea lies to the left, both tamed and restless;
we gaze outside – there shines a little moon.

In front of me the just-shaved necks of two
young sailors; they stifle yawns and shudders
and later, after some supple stretching out,
sleep innocently against each other's shoulders.

Then suddenly, dreamlike, in my window-glass,
flimsy and slight, rides the ghost of this bus
attached to us somehow, sometimes distinct,
sometimes drowned in the sea;
the grass cuts right through the sailors and I see
myself there too. Or just
my head, bobbing upon the water's surface,
the mouth moving as if speaking,
a mermaid, slightly amazed.
No end, no beginning to this journey,
no future and no past, all out of range,
only this present, long and split and strange.

BRASS BAND

The sky shone winking through the leaves,
as pale and pure as sharpened glass.
With manly force the horns were seized
and loudly confident, all brass,
the music squirted everywhere
among the trees, heroic, proud,
a less than timid music, loud,
without disguise, without digression,
music that gave its breathless public
a name for every feeling or expression.

And just as suddenly the clatter
hushed, two copper throats began lamenting ...
across the dark green water
two little ducks came swimming
as silent as a dream or painting –
The horns, suppressed, imploring,
seemed to be trying to ask them something,
to follow them with almost human grief.

A sorrow, warm and unexpected,
a deep respect for ordinary things,
an urge to sing along, out loud,
and then to weep about this song,
all flashed across my pampered mood.
I felt saddened, I felt good.

AUTUMN

In my own thoughts I'm never big any more;
more and more rarely do I think my true existence
will show itself and dare to be cured of death –
always coming closer, growing clearer.
Today I watched the sky, teeming with stars,
bleach itself out to a pure and deadly brightness.
I haven't freed myself from anything
and now there's no time left, or almost none.
A high and spacious wind is rustling through
the crowns of upright, standing trees; a deer
has just appeared, next to the black water,
and a low sun shines through the shore grass ...
This is the only answer I can find, the one
that would free me, if I knew how to translate.

CHILD IN THE LIGHT

Light in the white curtains
seaweeds of light along the wall
light-beaches on the ceiling.
And sparkling even more,
the little curious face
the eyes small pools of blue fire ...
small white fingers clutch
eagerly, from the sun,
hairs, so thin as to be invisible,
from the horse of Phaeton.

THUNDER IN THE MARSH

Next to the sleek, flat lake,
blue and pink as a moonstone,
stands an upright forest of reeds,
each stalk a green spear,
each spear slender and alone,
with a varnish of light, thin.
The shadow and light aren't moving.

Heavy in the sky hang harsh,
violet-colored clouds.
Nothing betrays the yellow crowds
of birds that populate the marsh.

Then, with a blinding light,
the sky splits open and slams shut
with one great clap …
As from a blacksmith's shop,
out of the reed-forest sprays
a spark-rain of rising birds,
swarm of a thousand fiery wings
beating on up into the somber heavens,
breaking free into a seething song.

My heart was suddenly white-hot
as if I too was forged upon that anvil
and I went through it anxiously
and came out new and strong.

FROM

THE PHOENIX BIRD (1947)

Dicky

16 April, 1942
10 October, 1943

"He has outsoared the shadow of our night"

PHOENIX I

During the war, I dreamt about a war:
a wooden airplane came down from the sky,
and taxied wobbling through the tall grass there,
then stopped: a groan, a song, a sigh.

As if from a sick ark, animals came, wounded,
one of each kind, dragging themselves to a tent
that I made resemble a small heaven, canopied,
with grass and trees and a glittering firmament.

On a long white table then I suddenly
saw a gray bird with a blue head, bright
like a vertical blue fire that burns fiercely,
on top of a hill as day turns into night.

Was he wounded, did I have to care for him?
Around my finger he clamped dry claws.
Soon the night passed and faded into morning,
a motionless dawn into which the sun rose.

And when I glanced down at my hands,
the finger he'd clamped was all blue
and wrote a verse while the bird burned ...
And he looked back, as if to bless me too.

PHOENIX II

This evening I was making a calm visit; words
swarmed like bees, and glittered among herbs;
there shot up from the grass that had concealed
him, and protected, a sort of bird,

a homesick thing, straight up and with a cry
that I thought everyone could hear.
And I knew him then, he who flew out of me,
who chose to make his nest within my fire.

Oh little phoenix, who lived in me too briefly.
I still see his eyes, blue fires,
feel his light weight on my hand, where he
perched, hear his wings sing as he flies away …

Don't rush this, don't scream with pain, oh hand,
write it down till your fingers are all burned.

CHILD

There was a light warmth above his face
like the earth at evening, just past sunset.
And his breath, like the wind in a curtain,
at his open lips went softly in and out.

He was life itself, almost visible without a shell,
and nothing but life, filled to the brim,
life without blemish or any heavy shadow
life raised up in a delicate cup.

How wide the passageway to life still spread,
how easy, with his ebb and tide, to reach …
How light and still and pure he stayed instead
alone with death on the deserted beach.

FAIRY TALE

for my mother and my little daughter

They listen, both, to her old tale,
and wonderful things come flying,
reflected in their wide eyes, floating
like flowers in an open bowl.

There's a soft tension in their being,
they sink into each other, lose their way
– the white hair and the blond –
believe it, do, believe it, do,
everything she says is true,
and nothing you read will ever hold such wonder.

DAPHNE

When I look up in the evening, the sky's no longer there,
and a great doubt hangs between the trees.
Darkness and rain rain down from the emptiness
with the unseen haste of underground streams.

Only my feet on the old ground
connect me to what exists,
something scarcely breathing, like the earth,
deep in her own being, compacted there.
The thing I still know for sure,
from which I'll nevermore be freed,
is this fixed and thickly branching grief.
My leaves stir in uncertainty
in which there's still a heavenly listening
and my roots taste so much darkness.

Deeply estranged from myself and my song
I listen, doubtful, to tone after tone,
disowning the tune, the beloved old melody,
disowning each thing that resembles attachment,
discovering scorn in the greatest of unities.
All that I see is separate, estranged.

I was watching one tree, most of the day;
it was raining steadily; leaf upon leaf
bent down, weighed by a drop,
dripped and rose softly upward ...
It rained like that, from leaf to leaf,
it rained the whole day long.

It rains ... I bend down and rise up
a little despairingly in this gray
state of mind. I'm so sick ...
Where is the heavenly music,
the unity of this earth in its singing?
All I can hear is that everything suffers,
sick from the sheer multiplicity of things,
lost in their absolute loneliness.

Between the low-ceilinged room with the big fire
and the out-of-doors, rising up high and frozen,
there is just a thin wall.
And I don't know which side I should belong to.

I stand at the window and smell the thin hoarfrost
coating the glass, something I've always loved.
The stars quiver in their invisible nets;
they're so light, so guiltless and free,
sparkling and moving within their proud laws.

And I've no idea what my own laws are;
I seek some distant, sure, inhuman sign
a way to escape this wilderness of pain,
myself too confused, too warm, too small.

What should I do with so much abundance?
"This is my life, this is my blood":
from every fullness the wafer remains;
almost invisibly, odorless, tasteless,
the perceived magic transforms inside me,
the red glow fading to a small white light,
stripped of all character, immaculate.

How can I breathe in this overpurified air
where all human warmth dies away?
How do I dare to speak, I who lack words,
and would not dare name anything except by sighs?

From birds, just the whisper of feathers,
or the finest grains of song, or the sound
of small dry feet beneath the dark roof.
How strong the reality, how weak
my instrument that points to everything
and tries to comprehend it. But it shrinks back
and the great truths of life
tremble like small stars.

In fear I seek to meet a godhead
without a face, one that would scald me,
would seize me without hands, without feet
I could embrace; one who, neither evil nor good,
destroys his creature even as I approach him.
So merciless and so true, so little father.

He maketh me to lie down in green pastures;
he leadeth me beside the still waters.

Now I will never again be desperate;
I feel the heave of the broad swell: death,
that like dark water under duckweed
creases my thoughts, secret and huge.

Around this breathing surface,
lightly and swiftly I walked,
whispering: let me live a bit more.
Now the wind opens the depths at my feet
and the blowhole grows ...
I loved you, oh green pastures,
my own heaviness helps me slide
to where death quenches my fires
in those still waters of old.

EVENING BY THE SEA

For my father

The beach was smooth and seamless
and narrow waves were breaking
from a thousand narrow mouths
that mumbled and then were mute.
The sea looked up, as if praying.
That's when I found you again.

Oh great, old, gray sea
such peace in so much restlessness,
one voice from a thousand small throats
conversing with the narrow coast;
unity out of so many opposites.
My old love, all my old trust,
so great, almost unbearable,
older than for my lover …
For the first time again I could see clear up to heaven:
how it rested calmly while exalting itself.

FROM

VISTAS AND VISAGES (1954)

PARTING

He left the house in the early twilight,
the doorstep was white and, drifting from the sky
came snow, glistening and fine as though trimmed from eyelashes,
snow that seemed to stay in the air, suspended and swarming.

The smell of snow and evening crowded into our heads,
and we grew pale and cold and pure as death itself;
when I looked at him he was distant and huge for a moment
and almost seemed to be making an urgent promise.

But when I came back into the warm room
there hovered a little cloud from his last cigarette,
and it spread itself with a kind of delicate haste, then turned,
and with a sweet gesture of wanhope and farewell
stretched itself out and then quickly vanished.

SOTTO VOCE

So many kinds of pain,
I won't recite their names.
Just one, this giving up, this separation.
It's not the cutting that's so rough,
it's being cut off.

Skeleton of a leaf, still beautiful,
butterfly-light, resting on the earth,
only now reveals its worth.
But between its suffering veins
there's nothing that might gladden:
laciness of your absence
that some pain holds together
over time, and growing greater,
more and more.

Poor, and ashamed to be so poor.

In the most ancient layers of my soul,
the ones that are rock and stone,
there blooms like a smooth, discolored fossil
the flower of your face, alone.

I cannot free myself from you;
nothing else blooms in that rock layer.
They are past and gone, all the old luxuries,
but you and I are together forever.

There are things that just trouble the surface;
the soul stays the same, underneath, and it gleams
like a pond on which leaves float
or a child's eye behind windblown hair.
You sing, and you listen to the way it sounds.

But there are types of grief
that change the nature of the song.
You are strung with very different strings
and no one knows this who has not lived it.

Oh child, with your soft white fingers
and the blue veins in your small temple
that meander like holy rivers.
Sleep my child, sleep.

TO VERSE

Between level-headedness and insanity,
vigilance and hopelessness too,
unbearable wealth and utter poverty,
I must belong to you.

Sometimes I stand in this balance, in doubt,
like an arrow, raised and quivering,
and then it's the way it is in a dream,
when you really need to scream
and no sound will come out.

PIGEON

There'd been a thunderstorm, the street was wet,
it lapped against the sidewalk like lake water,
and there a pigeon walked, with solemn gait,
and cooed just like a child, only sadder.

The sky above the park was getting light,
the trees stood green, stood self-contained, divorced,
each one as full of magic as a forest,
each muttering, enclosed, and raised upright.

I walked in the still street and gazed upon
the pigeon, his storm-colored wings,
his little feet as rosy as the dawn.

Nights, when I lie awake and wait,
wait for the light, so long,
I hear them bursting out, before first light:
the sources of all song.

Far off in the park, in deepest dark,
no more than a rapturous whisper floats,
then close at hand, from suddenly loud throats,
then silence again, and then so many heard,
until it all begins to run together too,
and the great silence is veined through
and the whole night is like a single tree
leafed with a thousand birds.

Then faster than the stars, at once,
the voices near and far are silenced.

Almost unheard, as from a still mouth drawn,
the silent breath of dawn.

HORSE SEEN AT THE STRASBURG CIRCUS

For Hans and Floortje

Horse that, ridden by a dream, without
bridle, without reins, came out
like a spring wind, the very first one,
plunging through bare streets and lanes,
rain and darkness pouring from his mane,
warm from himself, cold from the night.
Black horse on legs that flashed like lightning,
eyeballs rolling, nostrils flaring,
– oh loping out of where? where going? –
hooves that rattle like a racing heart,
about to burst, so quick, so swart,
horse that lifts himself up suddenly
with hooves that seem to touch the sky
blinding in his darkness and his wonder ...
and just as suddenly vanished,
like passion and its splendor.

44

CARILLON

Invisible cold invaded my warmer thoughts,
and grew rime-frost on branches, on the finest,
the youngest, those that had new buds.
When daylight came a morning wind arrived
and made them move, and thus produced a music,
a light one, like a carillon of glass.
It gleamed and tinkled, clear and bright and fine.
Then sun won out – the thaw, the clumsy stupid pain.

STAR

Tonight I saw a star for the first time.
He stood alone, he did not quiver.
Instantly, he pierced me through.
I saw a star, he stood alone, belief
made out of light: so young and from a time
before there was such a thing as grief.

The meadows lie unspoken in the light.
The cows, so often painted,
restrain, with a young, wet eye,
any account of their warm mystery.

MOTHER

Her self was like the sea, without the storms.
Bareheaded both, both with a broad foot.
Rising and falling on her tides, sometimes
perched like small birds upon her lap,
we would forget about her presence,
we'd rest, feel safe, look round.
Her voice was dark, a little hoarse,
like small shells rubbed together, and her hand
was warm and rough, like sand.
On her brown neck she always wore
the same chain, with a round moonstone
where a pale moon in a blue mist shone.
Filled as we were with her rustle and calm
we were always traveling, and always home.

WATER'S EDGE, TIME PAST

Hugging my skinny bruised knees I sat
and watched the slowly flowing water,
not even thinking or dreaming.
My head did not rise above the present.
I saw, and stayed the same: dead cats
stiff, flat, and grinning, like shadow puppets,
and rats with their scary coward faces
running out of their gray mud-holes
to plop quickly in the water, which chuckled,
and swallowed, and rearranged its creases.
And lizards too, motionless as hieroglyphs,
but pulsing with life behind brocaded heads
and their sudden disappearances – but the movement
was just as stiff, as if there was no moving –.
Nearby the hedge nettle, which doesn't sting or smell,
– fine hairs on the leaves, as on a human ear –
and I lay down there and sniffed my own hair
and the grass, stronger, and, stronger still, the ground,
and knew, eyes shut against the sun, that I existed.

TO A TREE

Sometimes you look out through your narrow eyes,
so summery, as though you look through leaves,
two narrow bits of blue, or so it seems,
inspired by the morning haze.
But please don't move. For who could bear it
if a tree pulled up its roots
and danced away?
Not me. And yet, you're made to move,
in lengthy lines, like steady music, simple,
and then again stand still, a slender temple.
And I can take that better.
I walked this evening in the garden.
The flowers were all white, the moon
had touched and moved her. I put my arms
around a tree. He was not large, his bark was hard,
but I could clearly feel a beating heart:
it was probably my own. Unseen,
I stood there in the wet and heavy grass
and felt that I had drifted into paradise.
Who can live there?

If you were a landscape I could walk in,
stand still and look around, take in the view,
and lie on the hard ground, saying nothing
stretched out, my face pressed to you …

But mostly you look like the sky overhead
where there's room for rain and light and cloud,
and like the wind, filling the space up there,
wind that nuzzles my hair,
covers my faces with kisses,
and never asks, and never promises.

Only what lives and has body;
all else is death-sweat, smoke, and dust.
And words should not exist,
nor images of divinity.
This evening the thin moon lay
tipped back and married to a star,
too emblematic and too far
because I could not touch it.
I want a word that can do sorcery
and conjure you to be with me
and hold me, *me*, thin moon.
I call you and you still don't come!
Since words words words have no sorcery.

WALK IN THE FALL

Along by squatting houses with hard, thick hair
over their foreheads, past forsaken gardens where
the beanstalks raise skinny fingers, as if in prayer,
– among wild foliage, from which rises now and then
thin smoke of fires and far off, glimpsed through
the hoarse, white-spotted red-stemmed grasses,
just the gleam of clean and thirsty-making water
in those small lakes one comes across in fall –
we went– oh carefree humming man –
we went along there in the summertime.
I walk alone there now, and slowly, and I stood
long on the narrow bridge, over the swollen stream
in which the grasses slowed and eddied as they sent
the water on a slant.
The land looked almost hollow:
the dark bottom of a lucid globe
that was completed by the crystal sky.
Far off among the woods
a child was talking to a dog,
so audible and yet invisible
it made me feel like someone who is blind.
Did all the longing and the restlessness of summer
lead to this lucid moment, keen and clear,
or has my heart gone cold; is this first frost?
The water gleams. Always, it seems, I thirst.

Just as a dog, drowning, bites his rescuers' hands,
my feeling bites the rescuing thought
that this distress will pass and that such nights
will one day fade away into past time.

The first to drown is expectation,
then hope expires. But remembering
fights the most stubbornly. Oh my darling!

SKELETON

Death is so often portrayed
as a skeleton, with outsized hands
and a grin through iron teeth
as if a rake had smiled.
I had to grow this old, and this amazed,
to understand that that is just more life,
stripped of its temptations
when one has gone long enough and far enough,
driven deeper with every step
into the quicksand of existence:
it's life that dares to stand this way before me.
– I laugh in response, he looks like a woman
who knows herself so married to her man
she no longer puts on her clothes for him
trusting triumphantly
that he does love her.

Now I know too, why I found something jolly
in that figure, that bare and shameless mouth,
the fragile cage of ribs, there where the heart
once hung and sang, a bird of light
caught in the tropics.
From all that was enticing about life
nothing's been saved but this transparency:
no song, no care, no love, no fire, no light.
Just this anonymous, iron, laughing face
and this cage, and these outsized hands.

AFTERTHOUGHT SOTTO VOCE

Perhaps I've grown fond of you, down to your very skeleton,
brutal, impertinent, and grinning life.
But it didn't happen *because* of those bones. Let
me catch my breath for a moment. I'll sing for you later
how often, how softly, your fingers caught hold of me.

EBB-TIDE

I pull myself back and wait.
This is not time that is lost:
every minute makes itself a future.
I am an ocean of patience,
lost in the thin and watery moment.
Suctioning ebb-tide of the mood
that stretches minutes and prepares the flood,
the flood-tide deep in its darkness, set.

There is no time. Or is there nothing but?

Just for a moment too long
I held my hand over the edge of existence
in the dark, fast water of time.
When I pulled him back across the quivering borders
it was as though he didn't belong to me any more:
he didn't grasp any longer, he lay cold in my lap,
he was missing his body.
Worse than death.

OLD

One dance, one dance with glistening eyes,
glowing cheeks, loose hands.
Then going to stand on the side. Feeling the wan smile
rise like mist on an evening meadow.
Cooling down slowly and noticing that
the mist is becoming snow.
Thinking wise thoughts then, laughing, lying,
profiting from the material loss?
Or jumping back into the revels again,
on stiff legs and with cold hands,
dancing and falling, covered in shame?
It doesn't help. Life is not pose,
nor is remembering, abstaining. Be still
and go away, and walk alone like an old wolf
and lick the last droplets from dry puddles.
Taste them thoroughly, it's your salvation,
and the faces you make are full of the memory
of earlier laughter. There's one more drop
of leaden existence, called the future:
the last gulp of undiluted, healing sorrow.

FIRE

Those who are young will barely recognize
the fire that, fiercely fanned by shame,
makes the old woman, besotted by love,
seek out the water.
Old Ophelia, thistles in her withered hands,
the cindery voice that still fancies singing.
But the water's the same and the old trees
have fresh green leaves and the thin song
stutters the same words. It's not pretty.
But the fire that this old torch has consecrated
cares nothing for beauty, time, or dignity.

FRAGMENTS

I

She walked the beach, as through a long-abandoned dwelling,
the paramour of some dethroned, great king,
until she sat down on a dark blue pier.
Stroking the stones, the broad blue blocks
covered with rough white pocks,
like gooseflesh on a frightened giant.
Gazing down and stroking, she sat like that and grew
used to knowing what she had thought she knew
already, deeply. As though she wanted to learn speech,
she put her flat hand like a deaf-mute on the beach,
felt in its throat a weakened humming,
watched the waves and moved her lips ...
But no sound came. The naming
stayed away.

II

It must get dark before I am reborn
and come out damp and little.
And she walked on some more, but it stayed light
and still there came no rain.
Then in the dunes she came upon a marvel:
a lamb, that had just drunk a tiger,
a bird that had just swallowed up a snake,
and a gentle one who ate the flesh of tyrants.
They all sat there, both speechless and besotted.
The bird addressed her then:
We went the wrong way, the back door of paradise,
and came to this strange country.
With her long tail, in which she stores the strongest poison,
the snake broke open that back door,
and now the circle's closed.
The lamb is spattered now with blood,
the bird can only sing with a split tongue,
the gentle one has murder in its blood.

III

Close by the coast, against a dune there lay
a woman, like the image of a god, that large,
intact; it was an image of tranquility.
She lay there motionless, her eyes wide open,
and what had seemed the murmur of the sea or wind
turned out to be a whispering, to which she listened.

Oh set me free, she whispered, looking up,
oh set me free, if need be, to be bad.
Let me speak loudly, even if I lie,
provide me food and drink, even if I vomit,
and lovemaking, even if I'm unfaithful.
I've fasted much too long and hate the smell of holiness,
I am locked up and hate my own security.
Like Gulliver I lie here, bound
by thousands of invisible, tough threads.
But will these great feet do no further wading,
and will my flat, extended, open hands
never again grasp something? Wasted lands.
Free me once more. I want to stand upright
and step aside. Then I will be less bad
than lying bound, with the deep hate
that fills the impotent, those who are all eyes,
smooth, noiseless, opal cannibals.

The image then grew silent
and tears appeared upon its eyelashes;
they soon dried up, to drift away like incense.
The face stayed dry and still, the throat
swallowed; a wide hand lay open on white sand.

IV

This is the next thing she found in her wanderings:
a naked feeling, with worn-out wounded feet
that could not fly away from that bare ground.
It sat and looked around, with open eyes,
and felt the air and felt itself, with fingers,
and snorted; but when she asked if it would like a drink,
it shook its head and clamped its mouth and shuddered.
It looked so cold, even in bright sunlight,
and dozed, and started, as if it dared not sleep.
When she lay down, as if she were a hill,
it came to her, as if to warm itself,
and shoved itself abruptly in her arms
and tore her breast, using its little nails,
and drank her blood and decked itself in red.
When finally it closed its eyes
its silenced mouth stayed slightly open.
The sun was gone; they lay there in the moonlight.
It was as though the hills began to whisper then,
or in the folds that opened, something soft
was moving. The air grew hazy, the stars less distant,
the dry hard ground, so like a fevered skin,
broke into sweat, a fragrance, and a salty wind, all mild,
curled the dry hairs of the sleeping child.

V

The sea was jumping up to the horizon
with wild, fresh flocks of gray-blue waves,
which buried her in foam and crashed together,
and of the rising tide nothing was visible but
fine lines, a jagged edge on the harsh beach.
More tender than the waving of a child's hand,
the moist blue coastline, gleaming, curved around.

That's what she saw when she climbed the morning dune.

CHILDREN COMING HOME

They come like big flowers,
out of the gathering dark.

Under the chilly evening air
that lightly drapes their cheeks and hair
they are so warm!
          Clasped
in the strong clamp of their soft arms
I glimpse the love, shadowless and full,
that lives at the bottom of their penetrating eyes.
It is not mixed with pity, which comes later,
and has its reasons – and its boundaries.

EXODUS

The kings remained kings
as I took their thrones away;
the slaves remained slaves,
as I struck off all their shackles.
Evening came on then and they left.
They could not live in me this way.

Those who could cry, cried,
proud and beloved to the final moment;
those who must stumble, stumbled,
loved even more and supported to the end.
The last to go, sucked through the sluice-gates, were
a whirlpool of horses, lashing their tails,
and when the dust had settled, strangely blessed,
along with the last rustlings of grit,
all I could hear was my heart, still beating,
as if it was running to catch up with them,
but I could not let it go.
In the dusk I watched as the gate disappeared,
and the high banks curled back like leaves,
and I stood alone, like a pistil.

Come! You who walk on bare feet ...

FROM

THE OLD COASTLINE (2002)

The wind has already begun
to sharpen your profile, muss your hair,
kindle darkness in your eyes,
the wind has already begun
to loosen the paper around me
unpack me, rumple and toss me.
There's something majestic and silent at work
in both of us here, at the water's edge,
our long legs humming like tuning forks
that resonate with the buzzing ground,
something we hear when, for a moment,
we stand still and listen, mouth upon mouth.

When you kiss me, your hand around my throat
as if I'd become a glass with a living stem,
beyond the tenderness comes a quick glimpse,
something that threatens my whole life with joy,
as if some giant, finished drinking,
will toss the glass across his shoulder,
and smash it on the ground
in order that no one else
can drink from it again, not ever.

Please don't look at me so sadly
with that crushed blue gaze of yours –
let me be separate for a bit
and let me breathe if I should start to choke
on this strange sense of being un-alone.
On never being given up for dead.
You need not fear my struggle
or let yourself be grieved about my pain.
I think that you don't really know me yet
whereas I am so used to being me –
and it's so difficult to make this child,
who has found things unbearable at times,
comprehend that you are really here.

PARTING

July, 1947

When your hand moves, my soul moves too –
and if you raise your eyes it fills with streaming light,
my love, my wing-beat, oh my gravitation.
I follow – wholeheartedly, completely captive,
each step, each gesture; your face's every alteration
alters me.
No, nothing's missing from our love,
except its full completion –
without which one can't breathe,
can't even live.

Here in your palace I'm too richly housed
and want to go back to my little room again,
and see nothing more, hear nothing more.
I want to be poor and empty, as before.
I-want-to-go-home!

It took a long time before her thoughts could move away
and divorce themselves from his clear image, until
it seemed that the hot chafing had started to heal,
and she stopped expecting him every day.

This has gone on for years: in the streets
a cheek or the back of a head will catch her eye,
or an elegant walk, and the present is swept away
amid the heart's crescendo of rising beats.

She feels no grief at this. The tears
that rise to her fascinated gaze just brim
to be tracing the tracks of an old dream,
paths that they traced for years.

Her heart, which lurches and then beats wildly
is like Odysseus' old dog: limps painfully
to the returning one, wagging to greet,
blindly recognizing his beloved foot
– oh if he comes, the house is empty, forgotten,
the dog is old and sick, and the food's rotten …

I used to obsess about purity.
What did I think it was?
Innocent, wading barefoot through cool grass.
Long walks on the beach. Being thin. And in politics,
far left. Lyricism was forbidden.
No thoughts about the future ...
and none so far, ever since,
thank God, and if I had no memory
I'd still be pure
and clean as rain
and just as drinkable, my dear.

CHILD

Four o'clock in the afternoon

During the conversation you've drifted away;
smiling vaguely, you untied your little boat.
You still look in our direction, rocking a little,
then you sit still and look straight up –
white face, neck a round white stem,
trembling a little. If God existed
and happened to glance down just now
he'd see you, like a little spot of light
rocking in a little cup of tea.

THERAPY HOUR E. S.

"What can we accomplish," he shouts hurriedly,
"We only have a quarter of an hour left."
He bends his long head, softly mossed, above
a wrist like a stick of cinnamon-stem
(heavily shackled by a watch-band with links);
his glasses go askew and with one finger
he pushes them back up the slope of his nose.
All business now, possessed, he grabs
paper and pencil, testing them briefly,
and then creates a rearing elephant,
tearing up trees and trampling huts,
and now – with a glance at me over his glasses,
a fateful look – he draws a black man leaning forward
at 45 degrees, who shoots and shoots and shoots.
Now the elephant is hairy with arrows,
his chest, his flanks, his tail.
His trunk not yet.
His trunk almost. He glances up again.
"The trunk almost got hit as well," he whispers,
and he draws an arrow with feathers right next to it.
"Better not the trunk, that's too pathetic.
But see for yourself: most definitely *almost*."

LOVE GRIEF

Tonight the stale breath of experience, bent
above the fresh and brokenhearted child
who sweats and cries salt tears and wrings young hands,
knows what it knows: familiar lullabies
will not suffice for this fierce sorrow, this new grief.
This is the hour, the end of childhood,
the gulf that marks out solace from its opposite.
They go their own ways now, oh yes,
parents and children, looking back and stumbling,
leaning against the old and trusted
but totally imaginary fence,
with useless hands, like battered cutlery;
they face a choice between a forced indifference
or trust based only upon love and hope
that things will turn out well. Or bearable, at least.

"Is this today, or yesterday?" my mother asks,
leaf-still, adrift on her white bed.
"Always today," I answer. She smiles, vague.
"Are we in Roden, or The Hague?"
And later: "Sweetheart, truth be told, I've gotten much too old."
I try to reassure her, precious snow-white astronaut
already having drifted too far out
who bravely volunteered to float in space,
to roam directionless, this way and that.
She needs – it is her S.O.S. – a way to get back home,
a child again, with all a child's pleasure.
And nobody brings her back the way she was,
nobody knows her. And now
she's eight years old again and learning French.
"*Bijou, chou, croup, trou, clou, pou, où* ...
Oh that strict teacher, vicious missus,
old Mademoiselle Who, what was her name?
Oh, I'm so tired, and it's all the same."

I wish I'd known you then, dear you,
my mother ... now my child too.

WEEKEND, MAY '66

So sweet you are, grown blond children,
out on the lawn this afternoon, laughing, sleepy, and warm.
So sweet, snow-white and wrinkled little mom in bed –
It's as though I put myself in shade, apart,
in other weather, yes, a different grim climate,
alone and afraid of the latent, pending tragedy,
seeing the shadow of the sharpened sword,
sick with impotence, mutely gesturing, wanting to avert
what's coming. This moment's briefer than a cigarette
in war-time: God knows
life becomes death and even the deepest love's
no use in creating duration. What's certain: pain.
I'm touchy and thin-skinned,
I who should believe and should be strong

INTERRUPTED S.O.S.
(TELEPHONE)

Oh don't drift farther away on the black water
your small dry voice blowing off in the wild
wind, your ice-floe apart from ours,
oh barely intelligible and desperate child.
The telephone sliced our conversation up
into white-paper crackling ghosts.
No undertones, silences, (sobbing?) arid sounds,
and I try ineffectually to warm
the miles of frozen air with my thin
long but not long enough arms.

MUTATIS MUTANDIS

A century ago, a young man would turn pale
if he saw your ankle and your veiled glance;
you'd lift your heavy skirt a centimeter
and blushing, turn your head so as to hit him harder.
He would go home and with a cut goose-feather
write fervently, discreetly, and with passion;
the first few months, the thing would go no further.
If all went well and if the affluent parents,
after a thorough inquiry, gave their consent to marry,
you would, with pounding heart and lots of questions, vague ones,
stand with him at the altar: respect and tenderness from him
and your own passion, well-controlled, would get you through.
Now you, my delicate and tender child, walking
in your high boots, wearing a mini-skirt,
a much-thumbed leather jacket round your shoulders,
board a packed train as both your parents,
resigned and anxious, learn to let you go.
Small and refined new instrument,
who in the crowd knows you and loves you?
Disguised as a swineherd, but inside
filled with a longing to love nobly,
beginning slowly and omitting nothing:
not the approach, not hesitation, and not loss.
What happens these days, as a party ends, the tumble
into bed, half scared, half startled by desire,
and in the morning going home again, immersed
in the uncertainties, the untrod paths:
maybe toward a beginning – or an end.

AFTERTHOUGHT

And yet I don't know if it's all that different
from former days – it's just been rearranged:
those letters and love poems were usually about
a goddess who had not become a mistress.
But how many women ever went on being worshipped *and* were comrade
partners and fellows, for better or for worse?
How many? Maybe not so very different.

MOTHER (2)

There was nothing, I thought, still think,
you couldn't do. Make pretty packages
that rustled with brown paper –
open the stuck jam jar, bandage wounds,
wire money, write condolence letters,
read out loud, speak five languages,
pull half-drowned dogs from the water,
and listen closely to long-winded stories.
But when the song began to end, you said:
I just can't do this, sweetheart, I can't do it.
And you meant dying. Struggling for hours
through the loose sand, searching for a handhold.
But you could do it after all, at last,
my dear one. And later, at the beach, I'll find you.
Please let me find you. You can do that, yes?

REBUS IN THE BUS

Here's who were sitting in the bus this morning
other than the driver whose pink cheeks
clashed with his beautiful red hair:
A rough old farmer with grey eyes,
his face under attack, and a restless kid,
deaf-mute, talking with his own thin fingers.
A woman in her fifties, gypsy more or less,
who got off at the trailer park;
she wore a leopard-skin coat and had small ears.
A Papuan family, from Dente by their accent,
so lovely and so ugly and so unconcerned.
I sat and listened and looked on
and said in all honesty and despite knowing better
that I could now expect at last "The Meaning"
of all those enigmatic lives together
would reveal itself to me, here in this bus.
But no – of course not. The one conclusion was:
I love people in a bus, I love grass
and air. I ride from Groningen to Roden.
I live for awhile. I don't understand it, mainly,
not even when "It" is offered up so plainly.

THE FOURTH WORLD

psychosis

Even without war, hunger, or discrimination, to be
obliged to beg, to be unfree,
be patronized, walk stooped from fear, in pain.
To be the last to occupy the smallest place,
not looking up, hoping not to be seen.
Answering, if one must, in a very soft voice.
Even humiliation is too much honor, too great a presence,
and evenings in the park, in the confused fog,
toes curled inside the shoes, feet turned to each other,
to wait – nothing can change, no help can come –
beyond the range of the mother-like trees,
to wait till the terrible bird inside
breaks open the shell and comes out.
And then to be two: the terrible bird and the empty shell –
without connection, just coexisting.
Then empty, unreal, but very needy,
to hold fast to anyone, embrace anyone
who reaches out, even with just one finger,
smiling down to his very bones, jumping from
one despair to another, like Eliza on the ice-floes.
Not even Jesus – who was abandoned by his father, god,
when he was on the cross, and whose complaint
was so modest as he hung there,
has known this loneliness, this bewilderment.

METASTASIS

Troy – Timeo Danaos et dona ferentes
For Fan

When you had beaten back their onslaughts,
the enemy seemed to have withdrawn,
bonfires were lit and a flood of celebration
broke out – the war was over.
The great gate demolished, the Horse came in,
and dispersed itself into a thousand strangers
whom nobody noticed at first. They never went away.
Finally trusting, finally vulnerable,
approachable at last, timid from happiness,
you were betrayed and destroyed. And *after* the battle.
From the inside out.

COMA

A sudden flood of tears
pours from her eyes, that do not see.
Natural phenomenon – or sign of grief?

Oh bitter hope for him, who like a falcon,
praying above her, searches in that landscape
for anything that moves, lives, happens.

But it's not there.

OLD AGE

I practice like a young bird on the edge
of the nest I must soon forsake
in little faltering flights
and open my beak.

Grandmother
                snow-white lace cap on
her calm sweet white-satin head
carried when she was in Holland, at home,
the smallest muff in the whole world:
inside a tiny bottle, no bigger
than an ampule. There was just room
for her hands. Plus one child's hand,
oh what a delicious nest of fur and
the very softest satin lining.
Then three hands were lying in her lap
inside a muff, "almost a whole cat," she said,
"minus one leg." Her eyes
were a constantly changing blue;
you could look into them as long as you liked:
as if you were seeing, through two small openings,
the calm sea on a summer day.

CET AGE EST SANS PITIÉ

Next door on the left – midships – there lived
a former sea-captain, widower, purple from drink.
His little daughter was spectacularly ugly,
so stunted and deformed and cross-eyed,
that all of us wanted to play with her
just to be close to something so sensational.
Her father made that impossible because
he offered us money to let her join in
which made it a job, so we didn't want to.
Also, she smiled so proudly, enigmatically,
that she felt dangerous – we didn't see the longing
expressed in her hanging out the window
with her crablike little arms for hours at a time.
But mother did – she often stopped a moment,
said something, asked something, inaudible,
and then one day admitted: She asked
if she might call me mother.
Surely you said no! Why? she said,
Naturally I said, yes, please do. And she was very happy.

SIMULTANEITY

Six in the evening, in the kitchen

The little dog with pricked-up ears,
the potatoes boiling on the stove,
the wooden tick of the clock – the sky
far and gray-blue and the jewelweeds,
tall as people. The pasture
with uneven tussocks and their shadows,
like drawings in a cave. And the knifelike light
that burns through the leaves, a glittering mystery.
And I – another creature, watching it.
It blends together and it doesn't change.
Oh Lord. I feel that something ought
to be made clear to me. That I've been granted time,
and yet, however overwhelmed I am,
something is missing that would help me say: this order,
however slipshod it may be: I see it, I'm awakened.
Forgive my deafness and my lack of seeing,
and hold me in your greatness – I am small,
but have, as well, too many tentacles
that grope in the different-being Being.

A summer meadow morning, very early:
carried upon a gentle puff of air
a tiny yellow butterfly floats by –
Lord, you should have stopped right there.

THE STOWAWAY

With every creature's birth, a voyage starts,
and death's aboard as cargo in the hold.
He makes himself familiar with the ship,
and penetrates the fibers of the wood,
the hull, the mast, the cables and the ropes,
the sails that squat all folded in the lifeboat.

The little children recognize him
and have no fear of him: they are
so short a time away from night
that they sailed out of recently
that they are hardly used to daylight.
The way that shadows have their part in light
so death lives on inside of every life.

FOR J. VERY SOBER

Just as my breath occurs of its own accord,
just as I rarely feel the beat of my heart
and hardly ever glimpse my face
even in the mirror,
so can I seldom, anymore, gone dumb,
put into words, my darling, the long love
that I no longer have
but have become.

A heavy and lead-gray eyelid
sinks slowly over the low sun
and he goes to sleep.
Who's dreaming? Snow
begins to fall.
Irregularly and steadily:
and through a veil
I see his glance, *one* blink,
drowsy and vague.

Outside the window, partly lit,
a long green leaf floats by in the night
and all my fear, stilled by the light and warmth,
breaks free, lit up, caught out.

This evening the wind is crying through a chimney, wild,
bodiless again, and lost, the child
who roams around inside me, restless,
until my death shall finally reconnect us.

Time, that streaming tide,
rushes so rapidly now
that everything's washed away.
Come trout, my memories,
leap now, and with fresh strength
and with the first wild scents,
against the current.

Back then it was birds at the window-pane,
now it's butterflies, like gossamer,
soundless and almost immaterial.
Oh it's time, high time, to depart.

Appendix

Theory versus Practice: The Case for Pragmatic Translation[1]

by David Young

Theoretical discussions of translation often seem to take place at such a remove from actual practice as to generate impressions of irrelevance and inadvertent comedy, especially in the reactions of working translators. But theory, of course, is not something we can toss aside. Even my opening sentence, doubting theory's efficacy for practice, has its own theoretical gist, generalizing as it does about the relationship. What does seem worth asserting is that any approach to practice that is too rule-bound or too ideologically grounded, that is not in itself pragmatic and open, will sooner or later prove problematic. A good translator, among other things, is a flexible performer, adapting to circumstance and opportunistic about possibility.

I can illustrate this, I think, by describing some recent work,

---

1   This essay first appeared in the Yearbook of Comparative and General Literature, vol. 54, 2008, published by The Department of Comparative Literature, Indiana University, and The University of Toronto Press in collaboration with The American Comparative Literature Association and The National Council of Teachers of English.

with a collaborator, on the twentieth century Dutch poet, M. Vasalis. My translation partner, Fred Lessing, grew up in Holland. He was a hidden child during the Second World War, and he and his family immigrated to the United States when he was about twelve. We knew each other quite well in college. Over the years, he has kept up his Dutch and he mentioned to me, when we went together to a recent college reunion, that he knew of an interesting poet who had not, to his knowledge, been translated into English. Being somewhat addicted to translation – it is how I read non-English poets I am particularly interested in – I suggested we experiment with a collaboration that by now has led to a sizable manuscript. His role is to translate the Dutch, more or less literally, and mine is to try to fashion an effective version in English. We then discuss the results and try to arrive at a final version.

I knew very little about Vasalis at the beginning. Her dates are 1909-1998. She was a psychiatrist and her pen name is said to be a Latin version of her maiden name. She published three collections in her lifetime, and a fourth appeared posthumously. She is widely read and very popular in Holland, but we have so far not found more than a handful of her poems in English, a shortcoming we have been happy to remedy.

Issues of rhyme and meter surround the practice of translating this poet, and what I have learned, I think, is to avoid too many preconceptions about how to respond to them. By this I mean that in reading the poem in Dutch, and absorbing Fred Lessing's literal and annotated versions, I try to get a feel for how much the formal elements meant to the poet in each particular case. It can be described as a question of priorities. Broadly speaking, I would say that in her early work Vasalis is much preoccupied with the traditional poetic features she has chosen; they have a kind of precedence that a translator cannot ignore. Her later poetry, on the other hand, while still employing rhyme, and loosened meter, shows her much more casual about those elements, a casualness that gives the translator more latitude of response. Poetic effects like off-rhyme, internal rhyme, assonance, and consonance, can be used to reflect this more casual formality.

It's also true, I think, that as a translator grows more familiar with a poet's body of work, he or she becomes aware of more options in the way that that work may be negotiated between one language and another. There is simply no substitute for having spent extended time in the presence of another poet's work, learning to trace the habits of thought and expression that the poet characteristically followed. Vasalis' creative process is by now much more familiar to both of us, as we have worked, separately and together, on some seventy of her poems.

I can illustrate her shift in emphasis, and my own considered response to it, I think, by use of an early and a late Vasalis poem. Readers will not need to know Dutch to sense the formality of this text – the first one, actually, that we worked on together:

DE IDIOOT IN HET BAD

Met opgetrokken schouders, toegeknepen ogen,
Haast dravend en vaak hakend in de mat,
Lelijk en onbeholpen aan zusters arm gebogen,
Gaat elke week de idioot naar 't bad

De damp die van het warme water slaat
Maakt hem geruster : witte stoom …
En bij elk kledingstuk, dat van hem afgaat,
Bevangt hem meer en meer een oud vertrouwde droom.

De zuster laat hem in het water glijden,
Hij vouwt zijn dunne armen op zijn borst,
Hij zucht, als bij het lessen van zijn eerste dorst
En om zijn mond gloort langzaam een groot verblijden.

Zijn zorgelijk gezicht is leeg en mooi geworden,
Zijn dunne voeten staan rechtop als bleke bloemen,
Zijn lange, bleke benen, die reeds licht verdorden
Komen als berkenstammen door het groen opdoemen.

Hij is in dit groen water nog als ongeboren,
Hij weet nog niet, dat sommige vruchten nimmer rijpen,
Hij heeft de wijsheid van het lichaam niet verloren
En hoeft de dingen van de geest niet te begrijpen.

En elke keer, dat hij uit 't bad gehaald wordt,
En stevig met een handdoek drooggewreven
En in zijn stijve, harde kleren wordt gesjord
Stribbelt hij tegen en dan huilt hij even.

En elke week wordt hij opnieuw geboren
En wreed gescheiden van het veilig water-leven,
En elke week is hem het lot beschoren
Opnieuw een bange idioot te zijn gebleven.

The importance of the regular quatrains is immediately evident, confirmed by the rhyme scheme (a-b-a-b, with the exception of the a-b-b-a third stanza, and the recurrence of rhyme sounds from the two previous stanzas [-oren and –even] in the final stanza) and the fullness of each rhyme. This foregrounding of traditional effects seems intended to create a tonal complexity with regard to the subject (the anarchy of the idiot's world and the order of the poet's recreation of it), and it seemed to me that, as a translator, I had no choice but to try to replicate it, despite the fact that exact rhyme and regular meter now have somewhat different values and meanings in English. At this point it would probably be useful to provide Fred Lessing's literal English version:

THE IDIOT IN THE BATH

With hunched up shoulders, squeezed together [squinting]
    eyes,
Almost trotting and often hooking in [tripping on/over] the
    mat,
Ugly and awkwardly bent [stooped] on nurse's arm,
Each week the idiot goes to the bath.

The mist that rises from the warm water
Calms [reassures] him: white steam...
And with each article of dress he sheds [that comes off him]
A trusted old dream seizes him more and more.

The nurse lets him slide into the water,
He folds his thin arms upon his chest,
He sighs, as by the quenching of his first thirst
And round his mouth there slowly glows a great gladdening.

His anxious face has become empty and handsome [lit.
    beautiful]
His thin feet stand straight up like pallid flowers
His long, pale legs, already lightly withering
Appear [lit. come] to loom like birch trunks through the
    green.

He is in this green water still as (one) unborn,
He knows not yet that some fruits never ripen,
He has not lost the wisdom of the body
And does not need to understand (the) things of the mind.

And every time that he is taken out of the bath,
And firmly with a towel rubbed dry
And wrestled [shoved ?] (back) into his stiff, hard clothes
He resists [pushes/fights back] and then he cries briefly.

And each week he is born anew
And cruelly [harshly] separated from the safe water-life.
And each week it is the fate allotted him
Anew to have remained a frightened idiot.

The translator looking for ways to reproduce formality will of course be opportunistic, noticing potential rhymes buried in the text, e.g. "steam" and "dream" in the second stanza. Gratuitous rhymes, e.g. "first thirst," will need to be expunged.

Here is what I eventually came up with. We've debated the title, which is a bit more idiomatic in Dutch, but finally settled on the literal version of it:

THE IDIOT IN THE BATH

Trotting and almost tripping on the mat,
Held by his nurse, unable to speak,
Shoulders hunched up and eyes squeezed shut,
The idiot goes to his bath each week.

Mist from the water rises, spreads,
Calms him and reassures: white steam …
Each piece of clothing that he sheds
Brings him back closer to a trusted dream.

She eases him in; across his chest
He folds thin arms, his breathing slows,
And he sighs, as if he had quenched a great thirst,
While round his mouth a look of pleasure glows.

His anxious face is handsome now, quite blank,
His thin feet stand like flowers – pale, serene –,
His long blanched legs, withered a bit, and lank,
Are like young birch trunks glimpsed amidst the green.

In this green water he has yet to happen,
He need not know that some fruits never ripen.
His body has the wisdom it requires.
His mind can lose the world and its desires.

And when he's taken out, and toweled dry,
And dressed again in stiff, hard clothes,
He fights and weeps, resisting with his cries,
That world outside, to which he always goes.

Each week he is reborn to painful matters,
Each week, for him, the same fate lies in store:
Harshly removed from his life-giving waters,
To be a frightened idiot once more.

There are compromises here, to be sure, some in the form (off-rhymes instead of full rhymes, a stanza that rhymes a-a-b-b) and some in the sense, but several Dutch readers have assured us that we've caught the flavor and feel of the poem successfully. Any translation is of course the result of hundreds, even thousands, of miniscule choices, and we do not guarantee that this version is our final one, but for the most part we feel we have created an English version that is a successful sibling to the Dutch original. One reader particularly admired the fourth stanza, both for its fidelity to the original and for its effectiveness in English. For me, the stanza that follows it was perhaps the hardest to accomplish and is, in retrospect, reasonably satisfying.

"De idiot in het bad" belongs to Vasalis' first collection, *Parken en Woestijnen (Parks and Deserts)*, published in 1940. If we turn now to the posthumous collection, *De Oude Kustlijn (The Old Coastline)*, published in 2002, we can compare her early and late styles. She is still something of a formalist, tying her poems together with rhyme, but the rhymes are less strict and occur somewhat sporadically. Meter, too, is considerably loosened, so that the movement of the poem feels more organic to its subject and mood, less governed by a predetermined pattern. This has meant, in practice, that I can explore analogous effects in English without necessarily feeling the kind of obligation to the formal pattern that I felt with respect to "Idiot."

Here is the Dutch for one of my favorites among her late poems:

GELIJKTIJDIGHEID

zes uur's avonds in de keuken

Het hondje met de opgestoken oren
de aardappels, die te koken staan,
de klok die houten tikt – de lucht
ver en grijs-blauw en de manshoge
spring-balsemien. Het weiland
met de ongelijke pollen en hun schaduw
als grotten-tekeningen. En het felle licht
dat door de blaadren brandt, een fonkelend mysterie.
En ik – een ander schepsel, dat het ziet.
Het blijft tesamen en er verandert niets.
O heer. Ik voel dat mij iets duidelijk gemaakt
zou moeten worden. Dat mij nu tijd gegeven wordt
en ook, hoezeer getroffen ook, iets aan mij schort
om werkelijk te kunnen zeggen: deze orde
hoe slordig zij ook is: ik zie het en ik ben ontwaakt.
Vergeef mijn doofheid en mijn blind-zijn
en vat mij in uw grootheid – ik ben klein
maar uitgerust helaas met veel te veel tentakels
die tasten in her anders-zijnde Zijn.

Even the look of the poem, in Dutch, signals a different attitude toward poetic composition and presentation. The precise and "finished" feel of the earlier poem has been replaced by an interest in process that is already evident in the densities and hesitations of the text.

Here is the literal version that Fred Lessing sent as we began work on this poem:

SIMULTANEITY (SYNCHRONICITY)

six o'clock [in the] evening in the kitchen

The [little] dog with the pricked-up ears
the potatoes, that are boiling (cooking),
the clock that ticks woodenly – the sky
far and gray[ish]-blue and the person (people)-high
jumping-balsemine.[2] The meadow (pasture, meadow-land,
     pasture-land)
with the uneven hassocks (clumps) and their shadow
like cave-drawings. And the bright (intense, sharp, glaring)
     light
that burns through the leaves, a glittering (sparkling) mystery.
And I – an other creature, that views (sees) it.
It remains (stays) together and nothing is changed (changes).
Oh lord. I feel that something should be made
clear (clarified) to me. That now time is given (granted) me
and also, no matter how badly hit (beat up ?), something that
     matters
to really be able to say: this order
however messy (sloppy, slovenly, slipshod,) it may be: I see it
     and I am awakened.
Forgive my deafness and my blindness (lit. being-blind)
and hold me in your greatness – I am small (little)

---

2   Common names include impatiens, jewelweeds, and, somewhat ambiguously, "balsams" and "touch-me-nots". As a rule-of-thumb, "jewelweed" is used exclusively for Nearctic species, "balsam" is usually applied to tropical species, and "touch-me-not" is typically used in Europe and North America. Some species commonly planted in horticulture have altogether more fanciful names, such as "Busy Lizzie" (the well-known *Impatiens walleriana*).

but equipped alas with much too many tentacles
that grope (touch, reach?) in the different-being Being.

The versions of my collaborator, I can testify, including his willingness to run down the botanical information, seem to have grown in authority and poise as we have worked together. They make my part of the process relatively easy.

Here is the version that I produced shortly after receiving the above:

SIMULTANEITY

Six in the evening, in the kitchen

The little dog with pricked-up ears,
the potatoes boiling on the stove,
the wooden tick of the clock – the sky
far and gray-blue and the jewelweeds,
tall as people. The pasture
with uneven tussocks and their shadows,
like drawings in a cave. And the knifelike light
that burns through the leaves, a glittering mystery.
And I – another creature, watching it.
It blends together and it doesn't change.
Oh lord. I feel that something ought
to be made clear to me. That I've been granted time,
and yet, however overwhelmed I am,
something is missing that would help me say: this order,
however slipshod it may be: I see it, I'm awakened.
Forgive my deafness and my blindness,
and hold me in your greatness – I am small,

but have, as well, too many tentacles
that grope in the different-being Being.

I opted for "jewelweeds" because that is the folk name I myself know them by, along with "touch-me-nots." In the second line I have introduced a stove, partly because I like the way its "o" links it to the words preceding and following it. In selecting the phrase "knifelike light" I knew I was taking a slight liberty with the original sense (sharp or intense light isn't necessarily knife-like), but I felt, again, that the sound combination was arresting and that the fact of the kitchen helped prepare a reader for the comparison. Vasalis might have agreed, if she liked all those long "I" sounds.

I took this version to a session with the Seminar on Translation at the Lily Library, and our discussion of it revealed something I had only been half-aware of: in the first half of the poem (lines 1-8) Vasalis avoids rhyme, as she sets out the details of the domestic world and the bewildering larger world beyond. In the second half (lines 11-19 after a kind of transition couplet in 9-10), which might be described as a prayer, she resorts to greater formality: not to a strict rhyme scheme or a regular meter, but to occasional rhyming that serves to help shift the tone and present a world that, while precarious in its unity, is ultimately more reassuring than the one in the first eight lines. She rhymes "ziet" and "niets" as a couplet, ditto "wordt" and schort" (and the off-rhyme, "orde"), framing that latter group with "gemaakt" and "ontwaakt." In her closing lines, the "zijn-Zijn" rhyme, a word-repetition, feels especially crucial.

I had already reflected some of these effects with the off-rhymes "it" and "ought," and "time" and "am," and with the interior off-rhyme group "another," "creature," and "together," but our seminar discussion made me realize that I also needed to address the closing rhyme (or repetition) as well. The solution was staring me in the face: where Vasalis had varied from her "-heid" pattern ("doofheid," and "grootheid") in order to achieve her rhyme by means of "blind-zijn," I had the same opportunity. Instead of "blindness," I could say something like "blind-being" (the literal sense) and set up the final effect. Here is what I finally decided on:

> Forgive my deafness and my lack of seeing,
> and hold me in your greatness – I am small,
> but have, as well, too many tentacles
> that grope in the different-being Being.

It's not perfect, perhaps, being a rhyme rather than a repetition and being a little weaker in effect than "being blind" or "blind-being," but it reflects her canny use of formal effects without, I hope, too much distortion of her original sense. The distant rhyme-effect of "small" and "tentacles" helps solidify the closing lines as well.

My thanks to the members of the seminar who helped me see the necessity of this revision. Meanwhile, the process continues. It takes place, I would venture, with a disposition to explore possibilities and opportunities while avoiding too much theoretical baggage, and with a hope that the process, faithfully followed, will sometimes, even often, yield fortunate results. It has made us, both Fred Lessing and myself, resolute pragmatists.

CPSIA information can be obtained
at www.ICGtesting.com
Printed in the USA
FSHW010231170419
57311FS